Y0-AUY-411

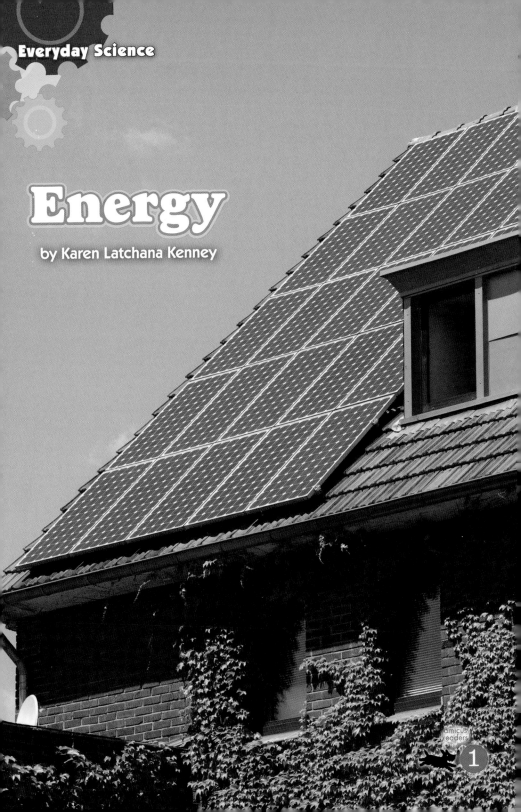

Energy

by Karen Latchana Kenney

Amicus Readers are published by Amicus
P.O. Box 1329, Mankato, Minnesota 56002

Printed in the United States of America at Corporate Graphics, North Mankato, Minnesota.

Library of Congress Cataloging-in-Publication Data
Kenney, Karen Latchana.
  Energy / by Karen Latchana Kenney.
    p. cm. -- (Amicus readers. Everyday science)
  Summary: "Describes how various forms of energy are used with everyday examples.
Includes experiments"-- Provided by publisher.
  Includes index.
  ISBN 978-1-60753-018-3 (lib. bd.)
  1. Power resources--Juvenile literature. 2. Power resources--Experiments--Juvenile
literature. I. Title.
  TJ163.23.K45 2011
  621.042--dc22

                              2010011281

Series Editor   Rebecca Glaser
Series Designer   Mary Herrmann
Production Designer   Bobbi J. Wyss
Photo Researcher   Heather Dreisbach

Photo Credits
acilo/iStockphoto, 1; Chris Scredon/iStockphoto, 6, 20 (m);
Dave Nagel/Getty Images, 13; David De Lossy/Getty Images, 5;
Dirk Ercken/iStockphoto , 16, 17, 21 (t); Emmanuel LATTES/Alamy, cover;
Grove Pashley/Getty Images, 15; marcpk/iStockphoto, 10, 21 (m);
Michel de Nijs/iStockphoto, 14, 21 (b); Monika Wisniewska/
iStockphoto, 8, 20 (b); Morgan Lane Photography/Shutterstock, 9;
Profimedia International s.r.o./Alamy, 7; Rob Walls/Alamy, 11;
Robert Lerich/Dreamstime.com, 12, 20 (t); Siri Stafford/Getty Images, 19

1222
42010

10 9 8 7 6 5 4 3 2 1

Table of Contents

AUG 5 – 2011

Beep, beep! The alarm clock goes off.

It's a big day!

Trista's class is going on a school trip today.

Trista turns off the TV.

She doesn't want to waste electricity.

Now it's time to leave.

electricity

Trista meets the other kids on the bus.

It is filled with gas and ready to go.

For science class, the kids will look for kinds of energy.

gas

Ava looks out the window.

The big traffic sign says school zone.

The sign uses solar power.

solar power

40

SCHOOL ZONE

11

Brandon plays his game.

Oh no! It stopped working.

His game needs new batteries.

batteries

Outside, Ben sees a big wind turbine.

The blades turn.

The turbine collects wind energy.

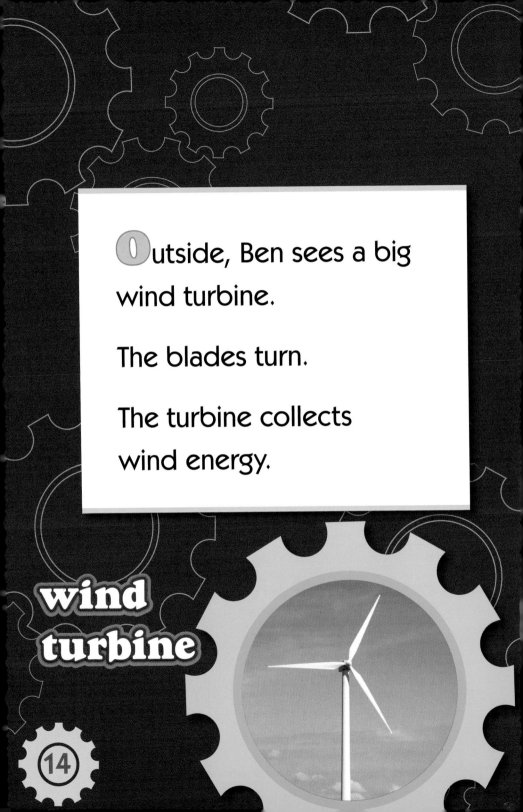

wind turbine

15

Leo points out a big tower with lots of steam.

It is the cooling tower at a nuclear power plant.

Energy is made inside the domes.

nuclear power

17

Max turns off his music player.

They are at the zoo.

The class saw many kinds of energy on the way.

Picture Glossary

batteries—containers filled with chemicals that make electric power

electricity—energy that is sent to buildings from power plants; Machines must be plugged in to use electricity.

gas—gasoline, a liquid fuel used to power cars, trucks, and motorcycles

nuclear power—power created by splitting atoms

solar power—energy that comes from the sun and is changed into electricity

wind turbine—a machine with moving fan blades that collects wind energy and makes electricity

Ideas for Parents and Teachers

Technology isn't just for engineers—we use it every day. *Everyday Science,* an Amicus Readers Level 1 series, introduces children to scientific concepts through familiar situations and objects. The picture glossary and photo labels reinforce new vocabulary. Use the following strategies to help your children predict, read, and comprehend.

Before Reading

- Ask students to name different types of energy. Record students' answers on the board.
- Take a picture walk through the book. Ask students to look at the photos and guess what is happening in each photo.
- Divide students into small groups. Ask them to discuss ways they use energy. Tell groups to share their answers with the class.

Read the Book

- Read the book to the students or have them read independently.
- Point out the inset and label on each spread. Explain that they show the kind of energy being used.
- Tell students to look at the glossary terms for more information.

After Reading

- Ask students to make a list of machines or objects that use each kind of energy mentioned in the glossary.
- Discuss why saving energy is important. Have students make lists of simple ways they can save energy.
- Try the activities on page 23 of the book.

Experimenting with Energy

Try This:

1. Stand in a dark room. Run a plastic comb through your hair 20 times. Touch the comb to the metal bottom of a fluorescent light bulb. Does it light up?

2. Lay a piece of colored construction paper in the sunlight. Put rocks on the paper. Leave it in the sunlight for two days. Does the sun's energy change the paper?

What happened?

1. Yes. A kind of electricity is made with the comb and your hair. It is called static electricity.

2. Yes. The sun's rays make the color fade. The solar energy affects the dye in the paper. Under the rocks, the color is bright. The rocks protect the dye under them.

Index

Web Sites

Energy Star Kids
http://www.energystar.gov/index.cfm?c=kids.kids_index

Energy Kids: Energy Information Administration
http://tonto.eia.doe.gov/kids/

Touchstone Energy Cooperatives – Kids Korner
http://cornbeltemc.apogee.net/kids/

U.S. Department of Energy. Energy Efficiency and Renewable Energy. Kids Saving Energy.
http://www.eere.energy.gov/kids/